T0071110

JOHN RUTTER

FEEL THE SPIRIT

A CYCLE OF SPIRITUALS

FOR MEZZO-SOPRANO SOLO,
MIXED CHOIR, AND ORCHESTRA
OR CHAMBER ENSEMBLE

CONTENTS

1.	Joshua fit the battle of Jericho	1
2.	Steal away	10
3.	I got a robe	16
4.	Sometimes I feel like a motherless child	23
5.	Ev'ry time I feel the spirit	28
6.	Deep river	38
7.	When the saints go marching in	44

MUSIC DEPARTMENT

OXFORD
UNIVERSITY PRESS

Feel the Spirit is available in two different instrumentations:

1. **Full orchestra**
   2 flutes
   2 oboes (oboe 2 doubling cor anglais)
   2 clarinets in A and B flat
   Bass clarinet
   2 bassoons
   4 horns in F
   3 trumpets in B flat
   3 trombones (2 tenor, 1 bass)
   Tuba
   Timpani (3 pedal timpani)
   Percussion (2 players: glockenspiel, suspended cymbal, clash cymbals, tambourine, claves, bass drum, drum kit)
   Harp
   Strings (1st and 2nd violins, violas, celli, basses)

2. **Chamber ensemble**
   Flute
   Oboe (doubling cor anglais)
   Clarinet in B flat (doubling bass clarinet)
   Bassoon
   Horn in F
   Trumpet in B flat
   Timpani (optional) and percussion (1 player: glockenspiel, suspended cymbal, clash cymbals, tambourine, claves, drum kit)
   Harp
   *Violin 1
   *Violin 2
   *Viola
   *Cello
   *Bass

   *One or more players on each part.

Scores and parts are available on rental from Oxford University Press or its appointed agent.

Feel the Spirit was first performed on 17th June 2001 in Carnegie Hall, New York, by Melanie Marshall (mezzo-soprano), the New England Symphonic Ensemble (director: Virginia-Gene Rittenhouse), and participating choirs in a MidAmerica Productions concert (Music Director and General Director: Peter Tiboris). The conductor was John Rutter.

Feel the Spirit has been recorded by Melanie Marshall and the Cambridge Singers, with the BBC Concert Orchestra, conducted by John Rutter. The recording is on the Collegium label (CSCD 523).

Duration: 30 minutes

FEEL THE SPIRIT

arranged by
JOHN RUTTER

1. Joshua fit the battle of Jericho

© Collegium Music Publications 2001. Exclusively licensed worldwide to Oxford University Press.

Printed in Great Britain

OXFORD UNIVERSITY PRESS MUSIC DEPARTMENT, GREAT CLARENDON STREET, OXFORD OX2 6DP

The Moral Rights of the Arranger have been asserted. Photocopying this copyright material is ILLEGAL.

17
B
mf
S.
Josh-ua fit the bat-tle of Je-ri-cho, Je-ri-cho, Je-ri-cho, Oh,
A.
Josh-ua fit the bat-tle of Je-ri-cho, Je-ri-cho, Je-ri-cho, Oh,
T.
Josh-ua fit the bat-tle of Je-ri-cho, Je-ri-cho, Je-ri-cho, Oh,
B.
div.
Josh-ua fit the bat-tle of Je-ri-cho, Je-ri-cho, Je-ri-cho, Oh,
(8)
21
f
Josh-ua fit the bat-tle of Je-ri-cho, And the walls come tum-blin' down. You may talk
Josh-ua fit the bat-tle of Je-ri-cho, And the walls come tum-blin' down. You may talk
div.
unis.
(mf)
Josh-ua fit the bat-tle of Je-ri-cho, And the walls come tum-blin' down. You
unis.
(mf)
Josh-ua fit the bat-tle of Je-ri-cho, And the walls come tum-blin' down. You
cresc.
8va

25
C
unis.
S.
A.
a - bout your king of Gi - de - on, You may talk a - bout your man of Saul;
T.
B.
talk a - bout your king of Gi - de - on, You talk a - bout your
C
mf
(8)
28
There's none like good old Josh - u - a At the
man of Saul, But there is
f
(8)
31
D
bat-tle of Je - ri - cho.
mf
unis.
Well, up to the walls of Je - ri - cho He marched
D
p cresc.
(8)

35
f
'Go blow those ram horns' Josh - ua cried, 'Cos the
div.
f
with spear in hand:
f
39
E
bat - tle is in my hand.'
mf
E
f
3
3
43
3
3
3
3

47
SOPRANOS and ALTOS
F
unis.
mf
Josh - ua fought that bat - tle,
F
mp
51
S.
So the Bi - ble say;
cresc.
And the walls come tum - blin' down:
A.
So the Bi - ble say;
cresc.
And the walls come tum - blin' down:
cresc.
55
S.
f
Great day! Oh, Josh - - - u - a
G
A.
f
Great day! Oh, Josh - - - u - a
T.
f
Great day! Oh, Josh - - - u - a
B.
f
Great day! Oh, Josh - - - u - a
G
f
mf

59
unis.
mf
div.
fit the bat - tle of Je - ri - cho, fit the bat - tle of Je - ri - cho, And the
63
H
walls come a - tum - bl - in' down.
f
Then the lam' ram sheep horns 'gin to blow,
67
Josh - ua com - mand - ed the
Trum - pets be - gin to soun'.
mf

70
slowly and freely
A tempo
Più mosso ♩ = 138
chil - dren to shout,
unis.
And the walls come tum - blin'
A tempo
Più mosso ♩ = 138
mf
73
unis.
f
mf
down. Oh Josh-ua fit the bat-tle of Je-ri - cho, Je-ri - cho,
mp
down. Oh Josh - - u - - a, Je - ri - -
I
I
77
unis.
Je- ri - cho, Josh-ua fit the bat-tle of Je-ri - cho, And the walls come tum - blin'
-cho, Josh - - u - - a, Walls come

81
J
(♪ = ♪)
mp
(♪ = ♪)
f
down.
Hal - le -
mf
unis.
cresc.
f
tum - blin' down, Oh Josh - ua fit the bat - tle of Je - ri - cho,
J
(♪ = ♪)
(♪ = ♪)
p
cresc.
mf
85
- lu - jah, hal - le - lu - jah, hal - le - lu - jah,
Je - ri - cho, Je - ri - cho,
90
f
Hal - le - lu - jah, And the
mf
cresc.
f
Josh - ua fit the bat - tle of Je - ri - cho, And the

94
K
p
walls come tum - - blin' down, down,
p
K
p
100
cresc.
mf cresc.
down, the walls come tum - - -
cresc.
mf cresc.
cresc.
mf cresc.
105
senza rall.
f
- blin' down.
f
senza rall.
f
sffz

2. Steal away

© Collegium Music Publications 2001. Exclusively licensed worldwide to Oxford University Press.

16
steal a-way, steal a-way to Je-sus; Je-sus, Oh Je-sus; Je-sus; Steal a-way, oh Steal a-
20
B
SOLO
steal a-way home; I ain't got long to stay here.
My Lord he calls me, he
-way; I ain't got long to stay here.
B
24
(SOLO)
Largamente
calls me by the thun-der; The trum-pet sounds with-in-a my soul;

27
dim.
I ain't got long to stay here.
C Tempo I
p
Steal a - way, steal a - way,
p
C Tempo I
dim.
p
31
poco rit.
a tempo
cresc.
steal a - way to Je - sus; oh steal a - way,
f
oh
p cresc.
f
poco rit.
a tempo
cresc.
mf

34
steal a-way home;
I ain't got long to stay here.
mp
dim.
p
steal a - way home;
A.T.B. Hum
steal home;
Oh
mp
mp dim.
p
mp dim.
p
mp
D
SOLO
37
mf
Più agitato ♩ = c.72
f
Green trees are bend - ing, Poor sin-ner stands a-trem-bling;
The trum-pet sounds
mp
p ma marcato
Lord, poor sin - ner trem-bling;
Hal - le - lu - jah,
Lord,
p ma marcato
D
Più agitato ♩ = c.72
mp legato
mf

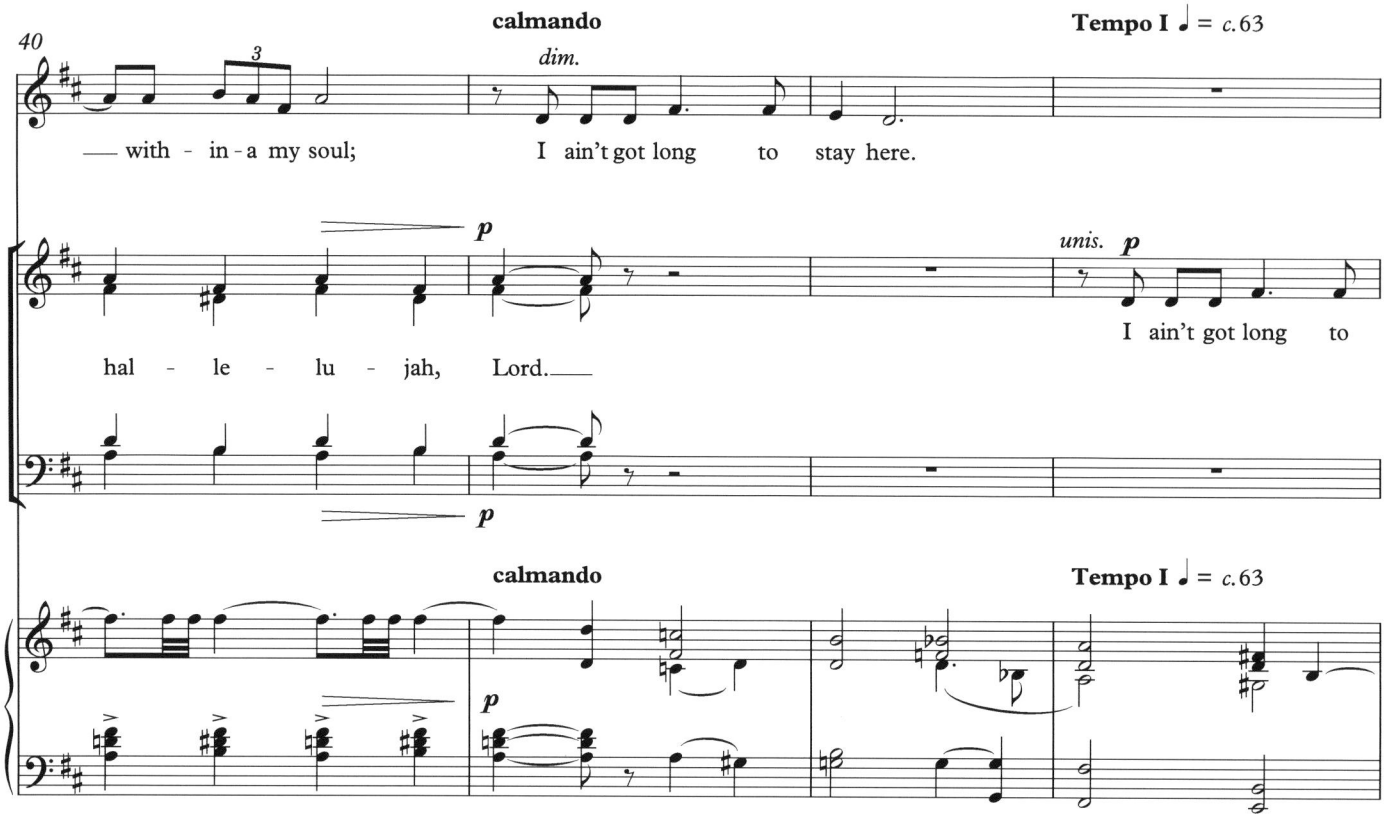
40
calmando
Tempo I ♩ = c.63
dim.
— with - in - a my soul;
I ain't got long to stay here.
p
hal - le - lu - jah, Lord.
unis. p
I ain't got long to
p
calmando
Tempo I ♩ = c.63
p

44
E
p
Steal a - way, steal a - way, steal a - way to
stay here.
E
pp

48
mp
mf
Je - sus;
Steal a - way, oh steal a - way home;
Steal a - way, oh
p
Oh steal, oh steal a - way home;
Steal,
p cresc.
52
F
rit.
I ain't got long to stay here,
I ain't got long to stay
A.T.B. Hum
pp
56
a tempo
rall.
here.

3. I got a robe

© Collegium Music Publications 2001. Exclusively licensed worldwide to Oxford University Press.

16
cresc.
f
hea - ven ain't go - ing there, Hea - ven, hea - ven, gon - na
mp cresc.
mf
I want to go to hea - ven, gon - na
and then I'm gon - na
mp cresc.
mf
cresc.
mf
19
B
shout all ov - er God's heav'n.
shout all ov - er God's heav'n.
B
23
TENORS
and BASSES
unis.
mf
I got - ta shoes, you got - ta shoes,
mp

27
T.
B.
All of God's chil-dren got-ta shoes;
When I get to hea-ven gon-na put on my shoes, Gon-na
31
C
mf
S.
A.
hea - ven,
hea - ven,
hea - ven,
T.
B.
walk all ov - er God's hea-ven,
hea-ven,
hea-ven,
C
35
Ev-'ry-bo-dy talk-in' 'bout hea-ven ain't go - ing there,
Hea - ven, hea-ven, and then I'm gon-na
Hea-ven,
hea-ven,
gon-na

39
walk all ov - er God's heav'n.
mf
D
Poco meno mosso ♩ = 108
43 SOLO mf dolce
Cadenza senza misura
I got a harp, you got a harp, All of God's chil-dren got a harp;
mp
CHOIR
Ah, ah
D
Poco meno mosso ♩ = 108
mp
sim.
Cadenza senza misura
accelerando
cresc.
48
SOLO
E Tempo giusto ♩ = 120
mp delicato
When I get to hea-ven gon-na
rallentando
f
dim.
mp
p

51
play on my harp, Gon-na play all ov - er God's hea - ven, hea - ven,
SOPRANOS and ALTOS
mp
Ah, ah,
55
hea - ven; Ev - 'ry - bo - dy talk - in' 'bout hea - ven ain't go - ing there,
(S. and A.)
ah,
Ev - 'ry - bo - dy talk - in' 'bout hea - ven ain't go - ing there,
58
rall.
hea - ven, hea - ven, gon - na play all ov - er God's heav'n. Oh
S. A.
p
hea - ven, hea - ven, gon - na play all ov - er heav'n.
TENORS and BASSES
mp
p
T. B.
hea - ven, hea-ven, gon - na
rall.
mp

Slow (quasi recit. but in tempo)
62
F
I got a crown, you got a crown, all of God's chil - dren got a crown;
mp
Mm mm mm
mp
F Slow (quasi recit. but in tempo)
p
Ped. * sim.
G Lively (tempo primo) ♩ = 138
66
S.
A.
mm
(mp) poco a poco cresc.
T.
B.
When I get to hea - ven gon - na put on my crown, Gon - na shine all ov - er God's
G Lively (tempo primo) ♩ = 138
p
cresc.
mp
69
mf
accelerando
cresc.
f
hea - ven, hea - ven, hea - ven,
f
hea - ven, hea - ven, hea - ven;
accelerando
cresc.

H
Poco più mosso ♩ = 144
72
SOLO
f
Hea - ven,
cresc.
Ev - 'ry - bo - dy talk - in' 'bout hea - ven ain't go - ing there, Hea - ven,
cresc.
H
Poco più mosso ♩ = 144
mf
cresc.
75
ff
(senza rall.)
hea - ven, gon - na shine all ov - er God's heav'n.
ff
hea - ven, gon - na shine all ov - er God's heav'n.
ff
(senza rall.)
f
ff

4. Sometimes I feel like a motherless child

© Collegium Music Publications 2001. Exclusively licensed worldwide to Oxford University Press.

25
cresc.
dim.
Some-times I feel like a mo-ther-less child A long ways from home, a
29
C
p espress.
long ways from home.
Ah
SOPRANOS
and ALTOS unis.
p espress.
Some-times I feel like a mo-ther-less child,
C
pp
p legato sempre
Ped.
33
Ah
Some-times I feel like a mo-ther-less child, Some-times I feel like a mo-ther-less child A
Ped.

37
A long ways from home.
long ways from home, a long ways from home.
T. B. Hum
p
cresc.
41
D
f
mf
mp
True be-liev-er, true be-liev-er, A long ways from home, a
True be-liev-er, true be-liev-er, Hum
p
dim.
45
(SOLO)
stringendo
long ways from home.
pp
cresc.
mf

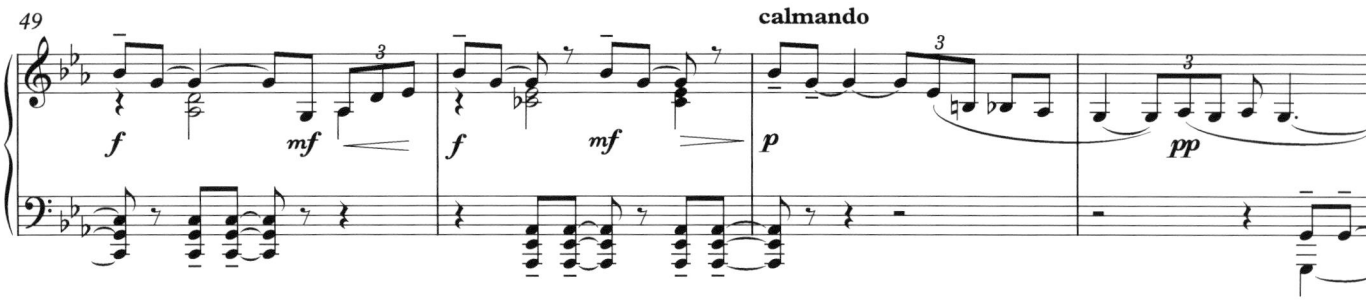
49
calmando
f
mf
f
mf
p
pp

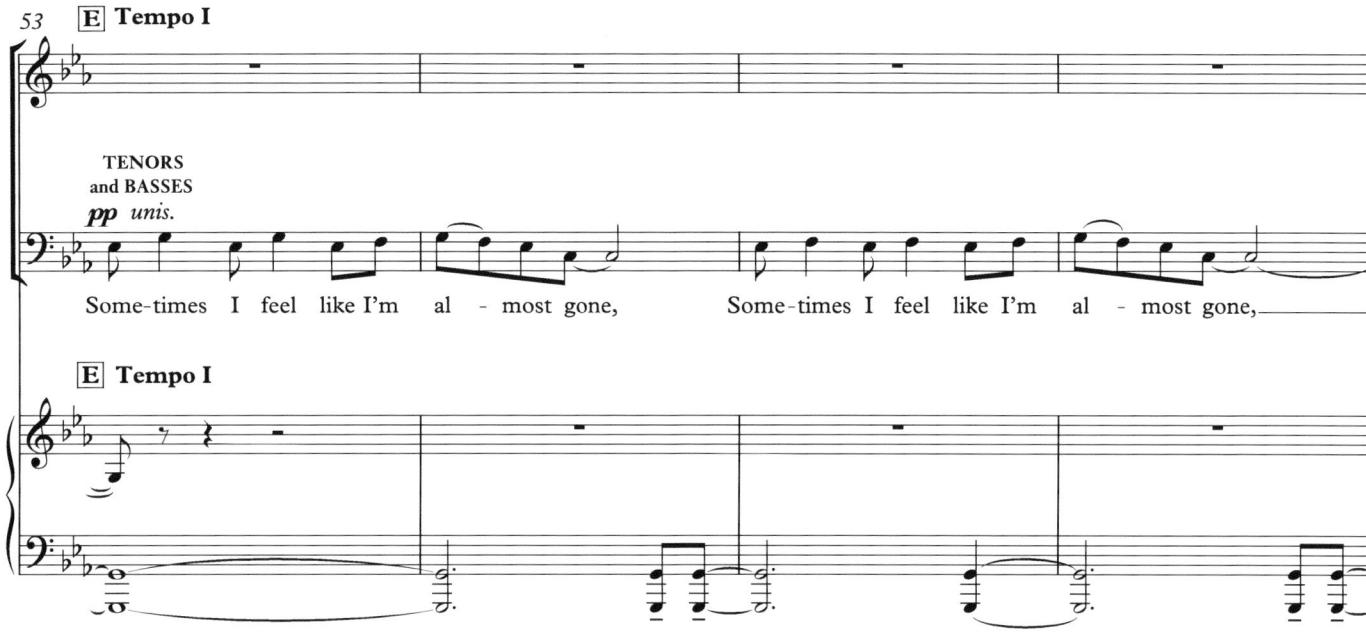
53
E Tempo I
TENORS
and BASSES
pp unis.
Some-times I feel like I'm al - most gone, Some-times I feel like I'm al - most gone,
E Tempo I

SOPRANOS and ALTOS
unis.
57
p
mp
p
Some-times I feel like I'm al - most gone, A long ways from home, a
mp
p
pp
I feel like I'm gone, Long ways from home, a
p

61
SOLO
F
f
mf
True be-liev - er, true be-liev-er, A
pp
mp
mf
mp
long ways from home.
Oh, true be - liev - er, true be - liev - er.
long ways from home.
mp
mf
mp
F
pp
p cresc.
mf
mp
65
rall.
mp
dim.
p
a tempo, un poco meno mosso
long ways from home, a long ways from home.
pp
Hum
B. Hum
pp
rall.
a tempo, un poco meno mosso
p
pp
69
mp
p
pp
(dim. a niente)

5. Ev'ry time I feel the spirit

© Collegium Music Publications 2001. Exclusively licensed worldwide to Oxford University Press.

B
Lively, but not too fast ♩ = 104
25
mp
pray. Ev - 'ry time I feel the spi - rit mov-ing in my heart I
accelerating
tr
(p)
33
pray;
SOPRANOS and ALTOS
unis.
mp
Oh, ev - 'ry time I feel the spi - rit mov-ing in my heart
leggiero
40
SOLO
mf
C
Oh, up on the moun - tain my Lord spoke; Out of his
I pray.
C
mp

47
D
mouth came fire and smoke.
SOPRANOS and ALTOS
unis.
mf
Oh, ev-'ry time I feel the spi - rit
D
54
mov-ing in my heart I pray;
Yes, ev-'ry time I feel the
TENORS
BASSES
mf
mf
61
S.
A.
in my heart I pray.
spi - rit mov-ing in my heart I pray.
T.
B.

E
67
SOLO
mf
Do Lord, oh do Lord, oh do re-mem-ber me; Do Lord, oh do Lord, oh
mp
73
do re-mem-ber me; Do Lord, oh do Lord, oh do re-mem-ber me
79
cresc.
f
F
mf
Way be - yond the blue in glo - ry: I got a home in glor - ry land that
mf
Way be - yond the blue in glo - ry:
mp cresc.
mf
cresc.
mf
F
mp marcato

85
out - shines the sun, I got a home in glo - ry land that out - shines the sun;
mf
p
Yes, my Lord:
mf
p
90
I got a home in glo - ry land that out - shines the sun, Way be -
f
mf
p
cresc.
mf
Glo - ry hal - - - le - - - lu - - - jah, It's way be -
mf
p
cresc.
mf
cresc.
mf
96
G
-yond the blue.
f
-yond the blue. Ev - 'ry time I feel the spi - rit
G
f

102
mov-ing in my heart I pray; Oh, ev- 'ry time I feel the
in my heart I feel the
109
SOLO mf
The Riv- er
spi - rit mov-ing in my heart I pray.
spi - rit mov - ing in my heart I pray.
115
H
Jor - dan is chil-ly and cold, Chills the bo - dy but not the
p legato
Oo Oo
p legato
H
mp

121
soul. And all a - round me looks so shine, I ask my
Oo
p
Oo
Oo
p
Oo
127
Lord if it all was mine.
I
Oo
Oo
I
Brass
f
133

139
mf
146
rall.
SOLO
J Andante, freely ♩ = 60
mp
I'm on the road to hea-ven now, you must take it too; I'm on the road to
p
l.h.
152
hea-ven now, you must take it too; I'm on the road to hea-ven now, you must take it
158
K A tempo vivace ♩ = 104
cresc.
too, Take it way be - yond the blue in glo - ry, yes, my Lord,
mf cresc.
f
yes, my Lord, Ev - 'ry
mf cresc.
f
K A tempo vivace ♩ = 104
mp
cresc.
mf cresc.
f

165
L
time I feel the spi - rit mov- ing in my heart I pray,
in my heart I
L

172
f
Yes, ev - 'ry time I feel the spi - rit mov- ing in my heart,
M
mp
mf
Ev - 'ry time I feel the spi - rit mo - ving,
p
mf
mf
M
p

178
cresc.
ff
in my heart, mov-ing in my heart, mov-ing in my heart I will pray,
cresc.
f
mo - ving, mo - ving, mo - ving in my heart I will pray,
cresc.
f
cresc.
f
(senza rall.)
185
p
in my heart I will pray.
cresc.
Sops. div.
ff
p
I will pray, in my heart I will pray.
cresc.
ff p
(senza rall.)
cresc.
ff p
ff

6. Deep river

© Collegium Music Publications 2001. Exclusively licensed worldwide to Oxford University Press.

18
unis.
p
Deep riv - er, Lord: I want to cross o-ver in-to camp ground.
unis.
p
p
B
SOLO
22
mf
Oh, don't you want to go to that Gos - pel feast, That
f
mp
Oh, don't you want to go to that Gos - pel feast, That
f
Oh, go to that
mp
f
B
mp
3
3
3
3

26
mf
dim. molto
poco rit.
pro - - mised land where all is peace.
mf
dim. molto
is
pro - - mised land where all is peace.
mf
dim. molto
poco rit.
f
mf
dim. molto
30
C a tempo
pp
p
mp
Deep riv - er, my home is o - ver Jor - dan, Oh,
pp
pp
C a tempo
pp
p
mp

34
mf
mp
p
deep riv - er, Lord: I want to cross o-ver in-to camp ground, I
38
D
want to cross o-ver in-to camp ground.
mp
dolce espress.
42
46
rit.
E a tempo
p
Deep riv - er, my

51
mp
p
home is o - ver Jor - dan; Deep
Jor - - dan;
mp
p
mp
p
54
SOLO
p molto legato
I want to cross o - ver in - to camp ground,
pp
riv - er, Lord:
pp
dim.
pp
molto legato
58
F
mp
dim.
p
Lord, in - to camp ground, in - to
mp
p

62
camp ground,
p
in - to camp ground,
p
65
pp
rall.
in - to camp ground.
mp p dim.
pp
Lord, in - to camp ground.
mp p dim.
pp
rall.
mp
pp

7. When the saints go marching in

Also available separately (978-0-19-343151-5)

© Oxford University Press 1990

19
(BASSES)
want to be in that num - ber, When the saints go march - ing
25
TENORS mf
B
And when the rev - - - e - la - tion comes, And when the
in. When the rev - e - la - tion comes, The
p
B
Cl.
31
rev - e - la - tion comes: Oh, Lord, I want to be in that
rev - e - la - tion, rev - e - la - tion comes, Oh, Lord, I want to
mp
37
num - ber, When the rev - e - - la - - tion comes.
be in that num - ber, When the rev - e - - la - - tion comes.

42
ALTOS
mf
C
Oh, when the new world is re - vealed, Oh, when the new world
mf
Oh, when the new world is re - vealed, When the
mp
When the new world is re - vealed, The new world
C
Tbn.
48
is re - vealed: Oh, Lord, I want to be in that
new world is re - vealed: Oh, Lord, I want to be in that
mf
is re - vealed, I want to be, Oh, Lord, I want to be in that
53
num - ber, When the new world is re - vealed.
num - ber, When the new world is re - vealed.
num - ber, When the new world is re - vealed.

58
S.
A.
T.
B.
mf
D
cresc.
Oh, when they gath - - - er round the throne, Oh, when they gath - er
D
(+Cl. and Tbn.)
cresc.
64
f
round the throne: Oh, Lord, I want to be in that num - ber,
throne, Oh, Lord, Oh, Lord, I
70
E
When they gath - er round the throne.
TENORS and BASSES
mf brightly
Hal - le - lu - jah, bro - thers,
mf

77
(T. and B.)
Hal - le - lu - jah, sis - ters! Hear the mu - sic go - ing round and a - round, While the
83
saints go march - ing up in - to glo - ry, Oh, hear those an - gel trum - pets
89
SOPRANOS and ALTOS
unis. f
F
And when they crown him King of Kings, And when they
mf
sound! Hal - le - lu - jah, bro - thers, Hal - le - lu - jah, sis - ters!
F
95
crown him King of Kings: Oh, Lord, I want to be in that
Hear the mu - sic go - ing round and a - round, While the saints go march - ing

101
num - ber, When they crown him King of Kings.
up in - to glo - ry, Oh, hear those an - gel trum - pets sound!
Cl.
(mf)
107
poco rall.
SOPRANO
mp legato
G Poco meno mosso ♩ = 92
And when the sun no more will
ALTO
mp legato
And when the sun
TENOR
mp
Hum
BASS
mp
Hum
poco rall.
G Poco meno mosso ♩ = 92
p
113
shine, And when the sun no more will shine: Oh, Lord, I
no more will shine, And when the sun no more will shine: Oh,

119
want to be in that num - ber, When the sun no more will shine.
Lord, I want to be in that num - ber, When the sun no more will shine.
Cl.
p
126
poco rall.
H
Ancora meno mosso ♩ = 69
div.
p
Oo
p
Oo
p
And when the moon
poco rall.
H
Ancora meno mosso ♩ = 69

132
Oo
Oo
Oo
Oo
has turned to blood, And when the moon has turned to blood:
Slowly, in free tempo
138
p
pp
Oh, Lord, I want to be in that num - ber, When the
unis.
pp
Oh, Lord, I want to be in that num - ber, that num - ber, When the
pp
Oh, Lord, I want to be in that num - ber, that num - ber, When the
pp
Oh, Lord, I want to be in that num - ber, that num - ber, When the
Slowly, in free tempo
pp

143
I
accel.
A tempo vivace ♩ = 104
moon has turned to blood.
moon has turned to blood.
moon has turned to blood.
And on that
moon has turned to blood.
And on that
Cl.
mp
cresc.
f
149
J
S.
A.
T.
B.
unis.
Hal - le - lu - jah, broth - ers, Hal - le - lu - jah, sis - ters! Hear the mu - sic go - ing
hal - - - le - lu - jah day, And on that hal - le - lu - jah
155
round and a - round, While the saints go march - ing up in - to glo - ry, Oh,
day: Oh, Lord, I want to be in that num - ber, On that

161
K
f
hear those an - gel trum - pets sound!
CHOIR 1
(optional)
Oh, when the saints
hal - le - lu - jah day.
f
CHOIR 2
(with audience ad lib.)
f unis.
Oh, when the saints go march - ing
K
167
go march-ing in,
Lord, oh, when the saints go march-ing right in:
in,
Oh, when the saints go march - ing in:
mf
Oh, Lord, I

173
mp cresc.
L
f
cresc.
Oh, Lord, I want to be, I want to be in that num-ber,
Oh, when the saints, Oh, when they go,
mp cresc.
f
cresc.
cresc.
f
cresc.
want to be in that num-ber, When the saints go
L
mp cresc.
f
cresc.
Ped.
sim.

179
ff
senza rit.
oh, when they march, they're sing - in' a 'Glo - ry, glo - ry, glo - ry hal - le - lu - jah!' Yeah!
(optional)
ff
ff
march - - - ing in.
senza rit.
ff
sffz